Be Happy Cartoons

Dr Stephen Katona

illustrated by Swapan Debnath

ISBN-10:1502730537
ISBN-13:978-1502730534

If I can stop one heart from breaking,
I shall not live in vain;
If I can ease one life the aching,
Or cool one pain,
Or help one fainting robin
Unto his nest again,
I shall not live in vain.

Emily Dickinson
1830-1886

The Healing Power of Cartoons

Cartoons are a fun way for our brains to absorb new ideas. Whether you flick quickly through these cartoons, spend time thinking how they relate to your own life, or just try spotting a few mice, you are likely to feel happier even if you think you are already happy.

The thinking part of your mind, of which you are aware, is called your conscious mind. It would be so easy if you could just decide to be happy. You can choose to smile more or pretend to look happy, but how happy you feel inside, depends on what your sub-conscious mind thinks. Reading lots of words can be tiring and whatever changes you decide to make, may be ignored by your sub-conscious. So how do you persuade your sub-conscious to be happy?

Try to respect how brilliant your sub-conscious is at making most of the decisions you make each day. Imagine how tiring it would be if you had to think how every individual muscle moves when you eat a meal, ride a bicycle or brush your teeth. Following your 'instincts' or your 'gut feeling' often leads to faster, better decisions and takes less energy. Brain scans of grandmasters playing chess shows they rely almost entirely on automatic parts of their brain. They often make their worst errors when they start to worry and think too much. Trust your sub-conscious more to make decisions for you.

The best way to talk to your sub-conscious is with your senses: sight, hearing, touch, taste and smell. Your dreams are your sub-conscious talking, and when was the last time you dreamt in words? These cartoons contain visual reminders of ways to feel happier, such as looking at family photos of fun times, watching 'feel-good' movies or a butterfly flutter by in the countryside.

Your sub-conscious finds it difficult to distinguish what is real from what is not real. It is important to expose yourself to the right sort of sights, sounds, smells and so on. For example, if you watch a horror film, or violent scenes on the news, your sub-conscious may remember events as if you had seen them in real life. Fortunately there are lots of ways to stimulate your senses in pleasant ways.

So, sit back, relax, enjoy looking at a few cartoons, and let your mind heal itself.

Contents

Thank you to my family and friends
for their support and inspiration.

I Can be Happy
I Will be Happy

Just a little every day
That's the way!
Seeds in darkness swell and grow,
Tiny blades push through the snow;
Never any flower of May
Leaps to blossom in a burst,
Slowly, slowly, as the first,
That's the way
Just a little every day.
"That's the Way"

New hope is fairer than an old regret.
"Forward"
Ella Wheeler Wilcox
1850-1919

Through the chinks and breaches of our prison we see such glimmerings of light, and feel such refreshing airs of liberty, as daily raise our ardour for more.

Edmund Burke 1729-1797

It is often a comfort to shift one's position and be bruised in a new place.

Washington Irving 1783-1859

6

Black holes are brighter than we used to think.

See the world in a brighter way.

Life is full of surprises. It's how you look at them that counts.

How wonderful this life, full of beauty,
We have plenty of time to stand and stare.
Time to stand beneath the boughs,
And stare as long as sheep and cows.

No gift is as precious as the gift of time.

Instead of dirt and poison we have rather chosen to fill our hives with honey and wax; thus furnishing mankind with the two noblest of things, which are sweetness and light.

Jonathan Swift 1667-1745

In the valley of the contented, the one-eyed man is happy.

Leisure
(a positive version of the poem by William Henry Davies)

A wonderful life this, if you are aware,
There's plenty of time to stand and stare.
Time to stand beneath the boughs,
And stare as long as sheep or cows.
Time to see, when woods we pass,
Where squirrels hide their nuts in grass.
Time to see, in broad daylight,
Streams full of stars, like skies at night.
Time to turn at Beauty's glance,
And watch her feet, how they can dance.
Time to wait till her mouth can
Enrich that smile her eyes began.
A wonderful life this, if you dare,
To spend some time to stand and stare.

Dare to be Happy

Once more on my adventure brave and new.
Robert Browning
1812-1889

The true secret of happiness lies in taking a genuine interest
in all the details of daily life.
William Morris
1834-1896

New hope is fairer than an old regret.
Ella Wheeler Wilcox
1850-1919

Use your fear to help you to change.

How I did respect you when you dared to speak the truth to me.

Anthony Trollope 1815-1882

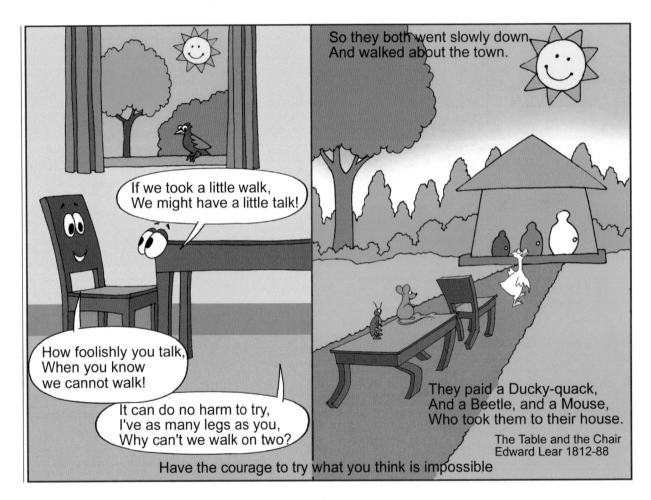

21

Why did the chicken cross the playground ?

Allow yourself to be happy.

I shall sleep, and move with the moving ships,
Change as the winds change, veer in the tide.

Algernon Charles Swinburne 1837-1909

Give a gift of great value.
Give a compliment to yourself and others.
Don't let its price tag fool you.

26

27

A hug a day keeps the blues away.

Learning a skill that seems unimportant, may bring
more smiles than you could have imagined.

Let go of the fear

Let go of the fear,
Of a startled young deer,
Listening for the sound of padded paws,
In case they come with sharp claws.

Let go of the fear,
That you've learnt to revere,
Question the choice of your brain,
To make you feel more pain.

Let go of the fear,
Cross a new frontier,
What makes you feel so harassed,
Could just be a memory from the past.

Let go of the fear,
Breathe deep the atmosphere.
To feel more calm,
Believe you'll come to no harm.

Let go of the fear,
Allow your health to re-appear.
Whatever you might feel,
May not be all real.

Let go of the fear,
Telling you to hear.
You have to believe,
It changes how you perceive.

Let go of the fear,
You've had for over a year,
If it makes your skin feel like a burn,
Or your tummy start to churn.

Let go of the fear,
And your soul will soon clear.
Don't let the pain in your head,
Fill your heart with dread.

Let go of the fear,
Then give a loud cheer.

Dreams of Happiness

What a joy it is to plant a tree,
And from the sallow earth to watch it rise,
Lifting its emerald branches to the skies
In silent adoration; and to see
Its strength and glory waxing with each spring.
Yes, 'tis a goodly, and a gladsome thing
To plant a tree.

"Go plant a tree"
Ella Wheeler Wilcox
1850-1919

Before we set our hearts too much upon anything, let us examine how happy those
are, who already possess it.
Francois de la Rochefoucauld
1613-1680

Go confidently in the directions of your dreams.
Live the life you have imagined.
Henry David Thoreau
1817-1862

Tie up the broken threads of that old dream.
Ella Wheeler Wilcox
1850-1919

It is perhaps a more fortunate destiny to have a taste for collecting shells than to be
born a millionaire.
Robert Louis Stevenson
1850-1894

Nurture your dreams.

Ever drifting down the stream
Lingering in the golden gleam
Life, what is it but a dream?

A Boat Beneath a Sunny Sky
Lewis Carroll 1832-1898

The River of Sleep
Ella Wheeler Wilcox 1850-1919

41

I never ask a man what his business is, for it never interests me. What I ask him about are his thoughts and dreams.

Howard Phillips Lovecraft 1890-1937

We should consider every day lost on which we have not danced at least once.
Friedrich Nietzsche 1844-1900

44

Edward Lear 1812-88

Spend time with a friend.

45

46

47

A mouse has a dream.

A mouse lives his dream.

48

Sometimes when I have dropped asleep,
Draped in a soft luxurious gloom.
Across my drowsy mind will creep
The memory of another room.

But still I love to wander back
To that old time and that old place
To thread my way o'er Memories track
And catch the early morning's grace
In that quaint room beneath the rafter
That echoed to my childish laughter
To dream again the dreams that grew
More beautiful as they became true.

"The Room Beneath the Rafters"
Ella Wheeler Wilcox
1850-1919

Be SEEN to be Happy

There was a sound in the wind to-day,
Like a joyous cymbal ringing!
And the leaves of the trees talked with the breeze,
And they altogether were singing.

"Greeting Poem"
Ella Wheeler Wilcox
1850-1919

The Blind Men and the Elephant
John Godfrey Saxe 1816-87

The blind men learnt from each other what an elephant looks like.

How baseless is the mightiest earthly pride,
The diamond is but charcoal purified,
The lordliest pearl that decks a monarch's breast
Is but an insect's tomb at best.

Beauty for all.

Earthly pride
Ella Wheeler Wilcox 1850-1919

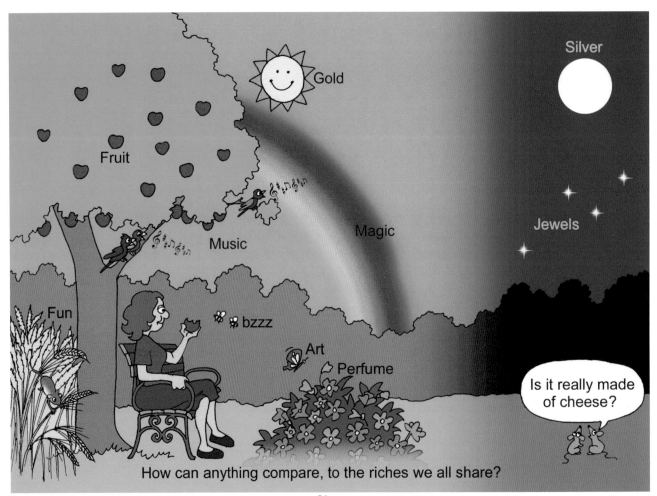

55

I am lonely, poor, and weak;
A little spot for a resting-place,
Dear flowers, is all I seek.

Come hither, poor worm, to me;
The sun lies warm in this quiet spot,
And I'll share my home with thee.
For a loving friend hast thou found in me.

At last the small cell opened wide,
And a glittering butterfly,
From out the moss, on golden wings,
Soared up to the sunny sky.

The home thou shared with the friendless worm
The butterfly's home shall be;
And thou shalt find, dear, faithful flower,
A loving friend in me.

Clover-blossom
Louisa May Alcott 1832-88

Be caring and loving, and you'll find many friends.

A dead thing can go with the stream, but only a living thing can go against it.

G.K.Chesterton 1874-1936

Feel the wind blow your worries away.

Feel each raindrop greet you.

Feel each snowflake with a sense of wonder.

Feel each ray of sunshine warm your heart.

Go outside and feel alive.

58

Hope is like the sun, which as we journey toward it, casts the shadow of our burden behind us.

Samuel Smiles 1812-1904

I go to Nature to be soothed and healed, and to have my senses put in tune once more.

John Burroughs 1837-1921

A Song of Life
Ella Wheeler Wilcox 1850-1919

The subtle beauty of this day
Hangs o'er me like a fairy spell,
And care and grief have flown away,
And every breeze sings, "all is well."

A Golden Day
Ella Wheeler Wilcox
1850-1919

For oft, when on my couch I lie
In vacant or in pensive mood,
They flash upon that inward eye
Which is the bliss of solitude;
And then my heart with pleasure fills,
And dances with the daffodils.

William Wordsworth 1770-1850

65

Finding Happiness

All we need to make us really happy is something to be enthusiastic about.
Charles Kingsley 1819-1875

You who are loudly crying out for peace,
You who are wanting love to vanquish hate.
How is it in the four walls of your home
The while you wait?
"How is it?"

Seeking for happiness we must take heed,
Of simple joys that are not found in speed.
Seeking for happiness we must take care,
For all the little things that make life fair.
"Seeking for Happiness"
Ella Wheeler Wilcox
1850-1919

Life is easier if you are adaptable.

What is a weed? A plant whose virtues have not been discovered.

Ralph Waldo Emerson 1803-1882

Time sometimes flies like a bird, sometimes crawls like a snail; but a man is happiest when he does not even notice whether it passes swiftly or slowly.

Ivan Turgenev 1818-83

The Rock and the Bubble
Louisa May Alcott 1832-88

Use your imagination to control your anger.

Where is the happy face ?

Where is the happy face ?

Be Smart without your phone.

Children at play are not playing about; their games should be seen as their most seriousminded activity.

Michel de Montaigne 1533-92

Come, cuddle your head on my shoulder, dear,
Your head like the golden-rod,
And we will go sailing away from here
To the beautiful land of Nod.
Away from life's hurry, and flurry, and worry,
Away from earth's shadows and gloom,
To a world of fair weather we'll float off together
Where the roses are always in bloom.

The Beautiful Land of Nod
Ella Wheeler Wilcox 1850-1919

76

Don't look for the flaws as you go through life;
And even when you find them,
It is wise and kind to be somewhat blind
And look for the virtue behind them.

Don't butt at the storm with your puny form,
But bend and let it go o'er you.

Don't set your force against
the river's course.

It is better by far
to hunt for a star.

As you go through life
Ella Wheeler Wilcox
1850-1919

77

What wisdom is greater than kindness?
Jean-Jacques Rousseau 1712-78

Play and have fun.

The Kitten and the Falling Leaves
William Wordsworth 1770-1850

One ship drives east and another drives west
With the selfsame winds that blow.
Tis the set of the sails
And not the gales
Which tells us the way to go.

Like the winds of the seas are the ways of fate,
As we voyage along through the life:
Tis the set of a soul
That decides its goal,
And not the calm or the strife.

The Winds of Fate
Ella Wheeler Wilcox
1850-1919

A Country Pathway
James Whitcomb Riley 1849-1916

I come upon it suddenly, alone
A little pathway winding in the woods
That fringe the roadside; and with dreams my own,
I wander where it leads.

Giving Happiness

Cast joy on the lives beside you.
Better the earth by growing in worth
With love as the law to guide you.
"What would it be?"
Ella Wheeler Wilcox
1850-1919

Smile upon your friend today.
Alfred Edward Housman
1859-1936

Those who bring sunshine into the lives of others, cannot keep it from themselves.
Sir James Matthew Barrie
1860-1937

A Holiday
Ella Wheeler Wilcox
1850-1919

84

Let the old life be covered by the new:
The old past life so full of sad mistakes,
Let it be wholly hidden from view
By deeds as white and silent as snow flakes.

A March Snow
Ella Wheeler Wilcox
1850-1919

85

What a world, if men in street and mart,
Felt that same kinship of the human heart,
Which makes them, in the face of fire and flood,
Rise to the meaning of True Brotherhood.

Brotherhood
Ella Wheeler Wilcox 1850-1919

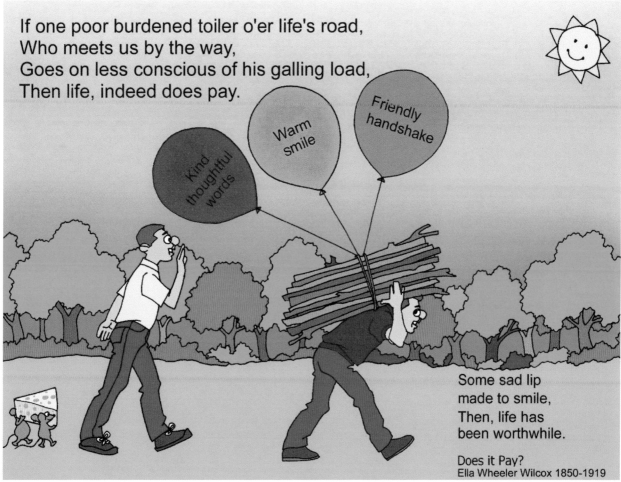

If one poor burdened toiler o'er life's road,
Who meets us by the way,
Goes on less conscious of his galling load,
Then life, indeed does pay.

Some sad lip
made to smile,
Then, life has
been worthwhile.

Does it Pay?
Ella Wheeler Wilcox 1850-1919

Being happy for a year is worth .... to me.

89

It is the generous spirit
Whose high endeavours are an inward light
That makes the path before him always bright

William Wordsworth 1770-1850

91

92

If we sit down at set of sun,
And count the things that we have done,
And counting, find
One self-denying act, one word
That eased the heart of him who heard,
One glance, most kind,
That fell like sunshine where it went
Then we may count that day well spent.

At Set of Sun
Ella Wheeler Wilcox 1850-1919

Power of Music
William Wordsworth
1770-1850

He works on the crowd,
He sways them with harmony merry and loud;
He fills with his power all their hearts to the brim
Was aught ever heard like his fiddle and him.

94

Are you a leaner, who lets others share
Your portion of labor, and worry and care?

Are you easing the load,
Of overtaxed lifters, who toil down the road?

People who lift and
People who lean,
Which are you?

Which are You?
Ella Wheeler Wilcox 1850-1919

The Camel's Hump
Rudyard Kipling 1865-1936

96

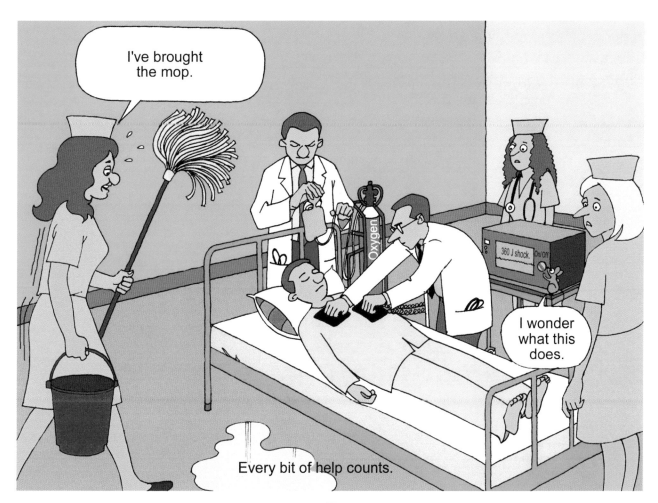

97

A door just opened on a street --
I, lost, was passing by --
An instant's width of warmth disclosed
And wealth, and company.

A door just opened on a street
Emily Dickinson 1830-1886

98

99

Giving Time

The best way to live,
Is to try to give.
Leave behind your greed,
To truly succeed.

Give an instant,
And be not so distant,
With a sunny smile,
For a little while.
Such a valuable gift,
Provides spirits a lift.

Give a minute,
If that's your limit,
To help another,
Like a devoted mother.
It shouldn't be rare,
When people dare,
To help those in need,
With a kindly deed.

Give an hour,
It's within your power.
Sit with a friend and laugh,
At an old photograph,
Of how your time began,
And share an exciting plan.
Pour sun on your future,
Close the wound with a suture.

Give a day,
Fill it with play.
Know a stranger well,
Bring them out of their shell.
Make it your mission,
To truly listen.
Showing genuine interest,
Is really simplest.

Spend your time
Helping others climb.

How soon we could gladden the world,
How easily right all wrong,
If nobody shirked, and each one worked
To help his fellows along.

I Am
Ella Wheeler Wilcox 1850-1919

Talking Happiness

Do you speak frequent words of commendation to those around you?
Do those you claim to love often hear you talking in love's language?

"How is it?"
Ella Wheeler Wilcox
1850-1919

The Butterfly that Stamped
Rudyard Kipling 1865-1936

104

The Butterfly that Stamped
Rudyard Kipling 1865-1936

Be the change that you wish to see in the world.
Mahatma Gandhi 1869-1948

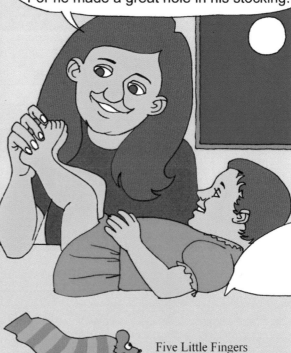

Five Little Fingers
Five Little Toes at Night
Ella Wheeler Wilcox 1850-1919

110

Under the snow in the dark and the cold,
A pale little sprout was humming
Sweetly it sang, 'neath the frozen mold
Of the beautiful days that were coming.

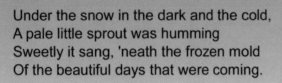

How foolish your songs

You are quite absurd

Birds, and blossoms, and buzzing bees,
Blue, blue skies above me,
Bloom on the meadows and birds on the trees
And the great glad sun to love me

From its prison, glorified,
It burst in the glad spring season.

The Tendril's Faith
Ella Wheeler Wilcox 1850-1919

Berty the budgie found Karen's hairdryer a little too powerful.

When bad things happen, try to see the funny side.

115

A Smile is a Wonderful Gift

A smile costs nothing,
But is an easy way to show loving,
A beautiful handout,
To take away doubt.

A smile opens eyes,
To star studded skies,
Lighting up the dark,
With heavenly sparks.

A smile is the butterfly,
A friend nearby,
Bringing colour to the day,
That before appeared grey.

A smile is sunlight,
To warm the night,
Melt frost from a heart,
And allow a new start.

118

A smile is the map,
To bridge the gap,
Between two friends,
And make amends.

A smile is a crashing wave,
Proof that you forgave,
Washing worry away,
To make all seem okay.

A smile can release a soul,
To make someone whole,
An easy way to build,
And feel fulfilled.

Let your smile grow,
Feel it's joyful flow,
Just make sure you find,
A smile that's truly kind.

Elf Happiness

It is easy enough to be pleasant,
When life flows by like a song,
But the man worth while is the one who will smile,
When everything goes dead wrong.
For the test of the heart is trouble,
And it always comes with the years,
And the smile that is worth the praises of the earth,
Is the smile that shines through tears.
"Worthwhile"

Sweep down the cobwebs of worn-out beliefs.
"Progress"
Ella Wheeler Wilcox
1850-1919

121

The Little Elf

John Kendrick Bangs 1872-1922

The 3 Directions of Respect

3 Give respect to others

1 Respect yourself

2 Receive respect from others

Self Esteem
Empathy
Value
Humility
Time

Build Respect

Out

We can all learn something from each other.

Take time to learn to love yourself.

All love that has not friendship for its base,
Is like a mansion built upon the sand.
When from the frowning east a sudden gust
Of adverse fate is blown, or sad rains fall
Lo! the fair structure crumbles to the dust.

Love, to endure life's sorrow and earth's woe,
Needs friendship's solid masonwork below.

Upon the Sand
Ella Wheeler Wilcox 1850-1919

At two o'clock in the morning, if you open your window and listen,
You will hear the feet of the wind that is going to call the sun.

And the trees in the shadow rustle, and the trees in the moonlight glisten.
And though it is deep, dark night, you feel that the night is done.

The Dawn Wind
Rudyard Kipling 1865-1936

I choose to compete.

I choose to feel calm.

Wash from our hearts and our souls
The stains of the week away,
And let water and air by their magic make
Ourselves as pure as they.

The busy mind has no time to think
Of sorrow, or care, or gloom;
And anxious thoughts may be swept away
As we busily wield a broom.

A Song from the Suds
Louisa May Alcott 1832-88

129

Strings in the earth and air
Make music sweet;
Strings by the river where
The willows meet

All softly playing,
With head to the music bent,
And fingers straying
Upon an instrument.

James Joyce
1882-1941

He knew at last that he had been a fool
To think of breaking the forest rule,
And choosing a dress himself to please
Because he envied the other trees.

Til the morning touched him with joyful beam,
And he awoke to find it was all a dream.

The Foolish Fir Tree
Henry Van Dyke
1852-1933

And always contented and happy was he,
The very best kind of Christmas tree.

The Child-World long and long since lost to view
A Fairy Paradise!
How always fair it was and fresh and new
How every affluent hour heaped heart and eyes
With treasures of surprise!

A Child-World
James Whitcomb Riley 1849-1916

I put my heart to school
In the woods, where the veeries sing,
And brooks run cool and clear;
In the fields, where wild flowers spring,
And the blue of heaven bends near.

Two Schools
Henry Van Dyke
1852-1933

Happy Times in Prominent Places

I like to put in a prominent place,
Pictures of my smiling face.

With so many happy times on the fridge,
Each snack helps me cross a bridge.

Friends smiling on my mirror,
Make the route ahead all the clearer.

Daring times on the kitchen wall,
Give me energy to climb a waterfall.

Vibrant scenes of nature provide,
Colour to fill the blackness inside.

There's no better use of space,
Than showing me a life to embrace.

Made in the USA
Charleston, SC
12 November 2014